Introducing the Middle East and North Africa

The region of the Middle East and North Africa forms a geographical bridge between Europe to the north and west, sub-Saharan Africa to the south, and Asia to the east. Its unique position has made it a highly contested area for thousands of years. Even now, parts of the Middle East and North Africa, such as Israel and the Palestinian Territories, remain in conflict.

As a region, the Middle East and North Africa is as diverse as any other region of the world, with a great variety of landscapes, peoples, cultures, and economies. There are, however, some broad similarities that make this region distinctive. The area is predominately Islamic in religion, for example, and Arabic is a language common to many of its countries. The area is also characterized by some of the driest habitats on Earth. Much of it is covered in deserts, including the vast Sahara desert that acts as a physical divide between the countries of North Africa and the rest of the continent, which is commonly known as sub-Saharan Africa.

The location of the Middle East and North Africa has long made it an important centre for trade between Africa, Europe, and Asia. Some of the world's oldest trade routes pass through the region, and key cities such as Istanbul in Turkey and Cairo in Egypt have grown up around this trade. Today, the region remains vitally important in the global economy because of its immense energy resources.

← The capital of Egypt, Cairo, is the largest city in the Middle East and North Africa. The Nile river cuts through this congested city of some 15 million people.

Spanning the continents

The 22 countries that make up the Middle East and North Africa form a unique region of the world because they span three continents – Africa, Asia, and Europe. The north of the region is marked by the Mediterranean Sea, which separates it from Europe. At the eastern end of the Mediterranean, Cyprus and Turkey (and sometimes Israel too) are Middle Eastern countries that are often also included as part of Europe. Indeed Turkey is currently negotiating to join the European Union (EU), a group of 27 European nations that share some common economic, political, and social policies. Cyprus became a member of the EU in 2004. Israel's inclusion in Europe is normally through cultural and sporting links. Politically it remains part of the Middle East.

Regional extremes

The most westerly country in the region is Morocco in North Africa. To the east, the region extends as far as Iran and Afghanistan, which share borders with Pakistan, China, and the central Asian republics of the former Soviet Union (Azerbaijan, Turkmenistan, Uzbekistan, and Tajikistan).

The most southerly point of the region is Yemen on the southern edge of the Arabian **peninsula**. This is just a short distance across the Red Sea and the Gulf of Aden from Eritrea, Djibouti, and Somalia in sub-Saharan Africa. Turkey is the most northerly country in the region.

Turkey's largest city, Istanbul, is built on both sides of a stretch of water called the Bosporus **Strait** – the dividing line between Europe and Asia. This makes it the only city in the world to be in two continents.

The largest country in the region is Algeria in North Africa, which covers 2,381,740 square kilometres (919,595 square miles). This is roughly one quarter the size of the USA, and almost ten times larger than the United Kingdom. The smallest territory, at just 360 square kilometres (139 square miles), is the Gaza Strip which forms part of the Palestinian Territories occupied by Israel. The smallest independent country is the island of Bahrain, at 710 square kilometres (274 square miles).

In total, the Middle East and North Africa covers an area of 12,647,170 square kilometres (4,883,100 square miles) which is approximately 9.75 percent of the world's total land area. However, the majority of this area is made up of inhospitable desert and mountain environments, so the actual habitable area of the region is considerably smaller. Population densities in areas such as the fertile Nile delta are extremely high.

Contents

Any words appearing in the text in bold, **like this**, are explained in the glossary.

Regional names

The countries of North Africa and the Middle East are sometimes grouped into smaller, sub-regions. The table below shows the most common of these, and the countries that are normally included in them.

Sub-regions of the Middle East and North Africa

Sub-region	Countries
North Africa	Morocco, Algeria, Tunisia, Libya, Egypt
Middle East	Bahrain, Cyprus, Egypt, Iran, Iraq, Israel, Jordan, Kuwait, Lebanon, Oman, Qatar, Saudi Arabia, Syria, United Arab Emirates, Palestinian Territories, Yemen
Arabian peninsula	Bahrain, Kuwait, Oman, Qatar, Saudi Arabia, United Arab Emirates, Yemen
Gulf States	Bahrain, Iran, Iraq, Kuwait, Oman, Qatar, Saudi Arabia, United Arab Emirates
Western Asia or southwest Asia	Afghanistan, Bahrain, Cyprus, Sinai (eastern Egypt), Georgia, Iran, Iraq, Israel, Jordan, Kuwait, Lebanon, Oman, Qatar, Saudi Arabia, Syria, Turkey, United Arab Emirates, Palestinian Territories, Yemen

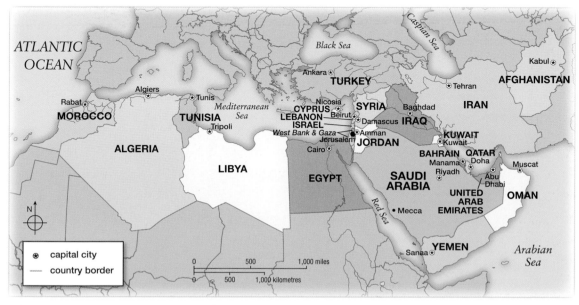

This political map shows the 22 countries of the region.
A table of all the countries is on page 56.

Ancient civilizations

Several of the world's ancient civilizations thrived in North Africa and the Middle East, as a result of trade and pioneering developments in agriculture. Mesopotamia was one of the earliest known centres of civilization in the world, dating back to 6000 BCE. Mesopotamia included the land between and around the rivers Tigris and Euphrates, that now forms part of Iraq and Syria. The name Mesopotamia means 'land between two rivers'. The Sumerian civilization was the first to develop in Mesopotamia. They invented wheeled transport, pottery skills, and the earliest known forms of money. By around 3000 BCE they had begun to build great cities such as Ur and Kish (in modern Iraq). The Sumerian civilization collapsed in 2004 BCE, under attack from another ancient civilization called the Elamites. Later in its history, the Assyrians, Greeks, Arabs, Mongols, and Ottomans were among other kingdoms or empires to control Mesopotamia.

Ancient Egypt, another early civilization in the region, thrived between about 3100 BCE and 332 BCE. On the narrow strip of fertile land beside the Nile river, the ancient Egyptians created some of the greatest architectural and artistic wonders ever known. These include the pyramids at Giza, close to the Egyptian capital Cairo, and the Valley of the Kings at Luxor. It was there that the ornate burial treasures of the young **pharaoh**, or king, Tutankhamun were discovered in 1923.

This map shows the countries of the region and their colonial rulers, in 1918.

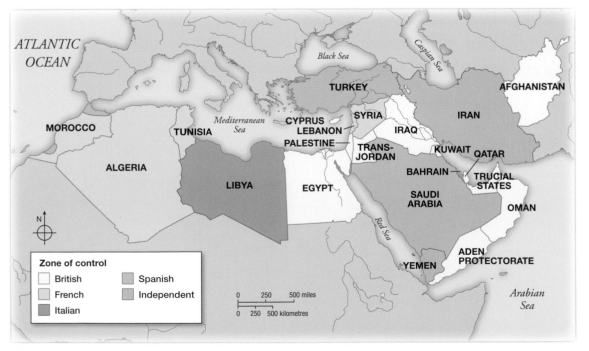

Empire and control

Many of the world's greatest empires have fought for control of the Middle East and North Africa. These included the Greeks under Alexander the Great, whose conquest of Egypt in 332 BCE ended the Ancient Egyptian civilization. By the time of his death in 323 BCE, Alexander the Great had created an empire that covered much of the region besides the Arabian peninsula and North Africa to the west of Egypt.

The Roman, Byzantine, and Ottoman Empires followed the Greeks, and continued to control much of the region. Under the leadership of Suleiman the Magnificent (1494–1566), the Ottomans controlled much of the present-day region. The Ottoman Empire began to collapse after its defeat in an alliance with Germany in World War I (1914–18). In 1918, its territories were divided up and many came under the control of the European victors from the war. Britain, for example, gained control of Jordan, Palestine (now Israel and the Palestinian Territories), and Iraq, while France took control of Syria and Lebanon. Britain already controlled many countries in the region, including modern day Bahrain, Egypt, Kuwait, Oman, Qatar, the United Arab Emirates, and Yemen.

The 20th century saw the end of the world's great empires, as the countries of the Middle East and North Africa gradually gained their independence. In many cases, the transfer of power from European colonial rulers to independent control was relatively peaceful, but in the case of Palestine negotiations about the British withdrawal from the territory resulted in disagreements and conflict that remain today. The Palestinian Territories remain the last state to be officially recognized as independent.

THE SUEZ CRISIS

Egypt gained its independence from Britain in 1922, but Britain and France kept control of the economically important Suez Canal. The canal, completed in 1869, joined the Mediterranean to the Red Sea. It was a vital link between Europe and Asia, as ships no longer had to make the long journey around the southern tip of Africa. In July 1956, the Egyptian president, Gamal Abdel Nasser, seized control of the canal for Egypt and sparked a brief conflict in which Israel, Britain, and France fought to regain control of the canal. The United Nations (UN) negotiated a ceasefire in November 1956, and the canal officially became Egypt's.

This event, known as the Suez Crisis, marked the final decline of European colonial influence in the Middle East and North Africa.

Wealth and poverty

In 2005, Israel, Kuwait, and the United Arab Emirates had an average income per person of over US$18,500 per year, more than in nations such as Portugal, Russia, and South Korea. By contrast, the average income per person in Afghanistan and Yemen was less than US$900 per year, making them some of the poorest countries in the world.

This variation in wealth is linked to two main factors. The first is energy wealth. Most of the wealthier nations have become rich because of their substantial oil or gas reserves. The second is political instability and conflict. Afghanistan and the Yemen have both experienced long periods of instability and conflict. This continues today, making it hard for their economies to operate normally. There are exceptions to this pattern, such as Israel. Israel is not energy rich, and has been in conflict with its neighbours for over 50 years, yet it is one of the region's wealthiest nations, with a high-tech economy and strong trade links with Europe and North America.

Quality of life

There are also major differences in quality of life across the region. Generally, the wealthier countries have higher standards of healthcare and education than the poorer countries. People in Afghanistan, Yemen, the Palestinian Territories, and Iraq have a lower quality of life than elsewhere in the region, as conflict and instability have disrupted these services. Their supply of basic needs such as water, food, and electricity can also be severely disrupted.

Within the region there are differences in quality of life by gender. In Egypt and Morocco, for example, there are only six **literate** (able to read and write) women for every ten literate men. Only in Israel and

WOMEN AND THE TALIBAN

The Islamic faith can have a strong influence on the rights and freedoms of women. In countries such as Turkey, Syria, and Iran, moderate forms of Islam mean women enjoy relative freedom in their dress and mobility. By contrast, the lives of women in Afghanistan when it was under the control of the **Taliban** were extremely limited. They could only appear in public if covered by a full **burqa**, and were not allowed to work or attend school. The Taliban's extreme version of Islam was heavily criticized by the international community. The Taliban were removed from power by a US-led international force in 2002. Today, women in Afghanistan have more freedom, and may attend school.

Cyprus do women make up more than a third of the total workforce. In Bahrain, Qatar, Saudi Arabia, and the United Arab Emirates they make up less than 15 percent. In the United Kingdom, USA, and Australia, by comparison, women make up 46 percent of the workforce.

Afghan civilians flee from fighting taking place in the town of Konduz. Thousands of people have had to leave their homes because of a series of conflicts in Afghanistan.

Natural features

The landscapes and climates of the Middle East and North Africa include some of the world's greatest extremes. The region includes the lowest point on Earth, the largest desert, and the longest river. It also experiences some of the highest temperatures and lowest rainfall of anywhere on the planet.

Two thirds of the region is classified as a barren or sparsely vegetated **ecosystem**. The world average is 16 percent. Most of this area is made up of desert, with the Sahara in North Africa by far the largest. The Sahara stretches from the Atlas mountains of Morocco in the west to the Red Sea in the east. It covers about 8.6 million square kilometres (3.3 million square miles), which is larger than Australia or the whole of Western Europe. About two-thirds of the Sahara is stony plains and barren mountains.

The region's other main desert is the Arabian desert, on the southern Arabian **peninsula**. It is known as Rub al Khali, meaning 'the empty quarter' and is the largest continuous sand desert in the world, at over 2.3 million square kilometres (888,000 square miles). It is connected to another desert, the Nafud desert, in the north of the peninsula. The sand dunes of these deserts are among the largest in the world, at up to 40 kilometres (25 miles) in length and over 100 metres (365 feet) in height.

← These stone buildings in Ait Ben Haddou, Morocco, are designed to keep people cool in the intense heat. They are built into the hillside, with thick walls and small windows.

Hot and dry

The climate of the Middle East and North Africa can be summarized as hot and dry. The region's deserts have less than 100 millimetres (4 inches) of rain in a typical year. Desert temperatures here are among the highest in the world, and in the Arabian desert regularly rise above 45 °C (113 °F). Coastal climates tend to be a little cooler, but are still hot for much of the year, and high humidity (due to evaporation from the seas) can make life very uncomfortable.

Further north, around the Mediterranean, the climate becomes similar to southern Europe, with hot summers and mild winters. Tripoli in Libya, for example, has temperatures of around 26 °C (79 °F) in July and 12 °C (53 °F) in January. Istanbul in Turkey has an average summer high of 24 °C (75 °F) and an average winter low of around 6 °C (43 °F). Rainfall is higher here than inland, and comes mostly in the winter. By world standards, however, rainfall is still low, with monthly averages rarely above 70 millimetres (2.7 inches).

Cool heights

Temperatures are cooler in the mountains, dropping by approximately 1 °C for every 100 metres (365 feet) above sea level. This is called the **lapse rate**. In winter (approximately November to March), temperatures in the higher mountains of Morocco, Turkey, Iran, Iraq, and Afghanistan fall low enough for regular snowfall. In fact, snowfalls here can be severe enough to isolate remote communities.

This map shows the key physical features of the region.

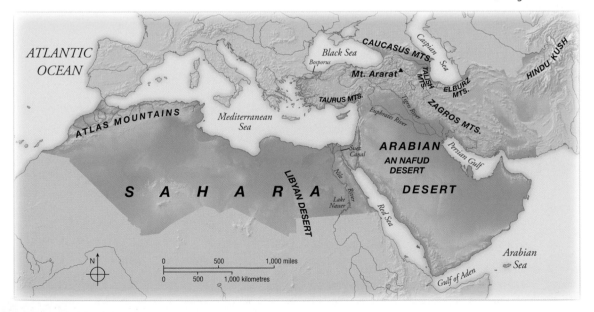

A camel train moves across the Sahara sand dunes in Morocco, North Africa.

GLOBAL WARMING

In a region that already has one of the world's hottest and driest climates, the threat of **global warming** is very serious. Higher temperatures would limit agricultural production and cause more heat-related deaths. Lower rainfall would put further pressure on already scarce water resources. Some experts believe that competition for water in the region could even lead to war. One of the areas most at risk from global warming is the low-lying Nile **delta** in Egypt. The farmland here is some of the most fertile in the world, and the area is extensively farmed and heavily populated. If global warming leads to rising sea levels, as predicted, much of this land could be flooded. Thousands of people would lose their homes and Egypt's economy would suffer greatly from the loss of its key agricultural region.

Water pioneers

North Africa and the Middle East suffer some of the greatest water shortages of anywhere in the world. The people living here have become expert in water conservation and supply. In Israel, for example, pioneering forms of high-tech **irrigation** have turned barren deserts into productive farmland. Saudi Arabia and other Gulf States are world leaders in **desalination** technology. This converts salt water into usable fresh water. In Libya, they are accessing ancient water stored deep under the Sahara desert (see box opposite).

Irrigation

Irrigation is the artificial use of water for growing crops, and it is essential to agriculture in areas with low or unreliable rainfall. The problem with irrigation is that it can be very wasteful of water. Traditional methods include flood irrigation, when land is simply flooded, and furrow irrigation, where water is channelled in furrows between the crops. These methods waste up to 90 percent of the water. It either seeps into the ground or **evaporates**, leaving behind salty minerals. Over time these poison the soil, making it useless for farming. Known as **salinization**, this is a major problem in the region. In Egypt and Iran it affects over 30 percent of irrigated land.

An automated sprinkler system in use in Galilee, Israel. This is one of many new forms of irrigation developed by Israelis to use their limited water supplies more carefully.

THE GREAT MAN-MADE RIVER

Libya is almost 98 percent desert and receives very little rainfall. In the 1950s, when scientists were exploring the Sahara desert for oil, they discovered enormous underground reservoirs called **aquifers**. These contained vast amounts of fresh water, some of which is thought to have been there for 38,000 years! In 1984, Libya began work on a project to extract water from these aquifers. Known as 'The Great Man-Made River', it is the world's biggest engineering project and will not be completed until 2025. Giant pipes, up to four metres (13 feet) in diameter are being buried beneath the desert to form a network over 1,600 kilometres (994 miles) long. These will carry water from the aquifers to where it is most needed along Libya's populated Mediterranean coast. As well as providing drinking and domestic water, the plans are to use the water to grow crops and turn the desert green.

Local people watch as water pours into the newly opened Salluq Reservoir, part of The Great Man-Made River project in Libya.

Israel has pioneered new, high-tech methods of irrigation. The best known is drip-irrigation, where small pipes with tiny holes in them drip water on to the crops. A computer controls when and how much water the plants need. This method has reduced water wastage to less than 10 percent, but is very expensive. It is only suitable for growing high-value crops, such as fruits, spices, flowers, and vegetables.

A scuba diver admires the coral in the Red Sea. This is said to be some of the best coral in the world, after the Great Barrier Reef in Australia.

Desalination

More than half of the world's desalination takes place in the region, particularly in Saudi Arabia which has access to seawater and plentiful supplies of cheap energy to run the desalination plants (desalination uses a lot of energy). Saudi Arabia, the United Arab Emirates, Kuwait, Libya, Qatar, Iran, Bahrain, Iraq, and Algeria are the biggest users of desalination.

Rivers

The Nile is the world's longest river, ending its 6,670-kilometre (4,145-mile) journey by cutting through the Sahara desert in Egypt. The Nile's flow is controlled by the Aswan High Dam, which was completed in 1970 to generate electricity and provide water for irrigation.

The Euphrates and Tigris are the region's other major rivers. The Euphrates is about 2,780 kilometres (1,727 miles) long, the Tigris is about 1,800 kilometres (1,118 miles) long. Both rivers originate in the mountains of eastern Turkey, and flow southeasterly through Syria and Iraq before reaching the Arabian Sea. The rivers unite near Basra in Iraq, and are then known as the Shatt al-Arab.

The Tigris and Euphrates have been the cause of considerable tension in recent years because of Turkish plans to capture and use their waters. The Southeastern Anatolia Project (abbreviated to GAP in Turkish) will involve building 22 dams across the Tigris and Euphrates by 2010. These dams will generate electricity, provide water for irrigation, and create lakes for fish-farming. Syria and Iraq depend on the Tigris and Euphrates for water, and are concerned that the GAP project will reduce their flow.

THE DEAD SEA

The Dead Sea, between Jordan and Israel and the Palestinian Territories, is a very salty lake in the bottom of the Jordan valley. At 400 metres (1,312 feet) below sea level, it is the lowest point on Earth. The salts of the Dead Sea are used by the chemical and cosmetics industries. They are collected by allowing water from the sea to evaporate, leaving the salts behind. This, combined with a reduction of water entering the Dead Sea, is causing the shoreline to retreat by up to 1 metre (3 feet) every year.

On the eastern shore of the Dead Sea in Jordan, the shoreline has retreated leaving behind heavy deposits of salt.

Seas and oceans

The coastline of the region stretches from the Atlantic Ocean off Morocco through the Mediterranean Sea, Red Sea, and Persian Gulf, to the Arabian Sea off Oman. Only Afghanistan lacks any coastline. Coasts have long been important for trade and fishing, and for this reason are quite heavily populated. The region's coasts also attract tourists, as in Tunisia and the Sinai peninsula in Egypt. Sinai has the added advantage of some of the world's best coral reefs, close to shore in the Red Sea. These attract divers from across the world.

The region also has three inland seas – the Black Sea, the Caspian Sea and the Dead Sea. The Black Sea, to the north of Turkey, is connected to the Mediterranean by the Bosporus **Strait**. The Caspian Sea is an inland salty lake to the north of Iran. It is the world's largest lake, covering 370,992 square kilometres (143,240 square miles), and has large reserves of oil and gas beneath its waters.

Mountains and highlands

The main mountains in the Middle East and North Africa are in its western and eastern extremes. In the west Morocco, Algeria, and Tunisia share the Atlas Mountains. Their highest point is the mountain Jebel Toubkal (4,165 metres/13,665 feet), south of Marrakech. The Atlas Mountains are divided into several sub-groups, but together extend for about 2,400 kilometres (1,490 miles) across northwest Africa. In the east there are several mountain groups. The Taurus Mountains in Turkey rise to 5,137 metres (16,854 feet) at Mount Ararat in the extreme east. Further east, Iran has the Zagros, Talish, and Elburz mountain groups. The Zagros range runs along the border with Iraq, and reaches a maximum altitude of about 4,500 metres (14,764 feet). The Talish and Elburz mountains skirt the shores of the Caspian Sea. Their highest point is Mount Kuh-e Damavand (5,671 metres/18,605 feet), close to the capital Tehran. The Hindu Kush in Afghanistan has the region's highest mountains, rising to 7,485 metres (24,557 feet) at Mount Nowshak, on the border with Pakistan.

As well as the mountain ranges, there are major highland and mountainous areas bordering the Red Sea in Egypt, Saudi Arabia, and Yemen. Much of Jordan, Israel, Lebanon, and Syria also consists of highlands and smaller mountains.

Fragile Earth

Parts of North Africa and the Middle East are at high risk from earthquakes. In October 1992, around 500 people were killed and 4,000 injured when an earthquake struck Cairo, the biggest city in the region. Thousands of buildings were damaged, especially those that had been built rapidly to house the city's growing population. In Turkey Istanbul, a city of over 10 million people, is in an area where experts predict a major earthquake is highly likely. The last major quakes struck Turkey in 1999, when two quakes in August and November killed over 17,500 people and left thousands more homeless.

Iran is another high-risk earthquake area. In December 2003, a powerful earthquake in southeastern Iran destroyed around 70 percent of the buildings in the ancient city of Bam. Around 27,000 people were killed, and tens of thousands were injured or left homeless. These figures are relatively low, however, compared with the damage and loss of life that would be caused by a major quake hitting Istanbul. The Iranian capital, Tehran, is in a risk zone, and following the earthquake in Bam some government officials even suggested moving it.

MOUNTAINS OF WAR

The mountains of the Hindu Kush in Afghanistan are especially rugged and isolated, so they have been favoured by armed groups (**militias**) involved in Afghanistan's long and complex history of conflict. The mountains hide them from the authorities or enemy forces. In 2001, when the USA and United Kingdom led an international force into Afghanistan to overthrow the Taliban government, many of the Taliban and their supporters fled into the mountains. These mountains are also thought to be used by the **terrorist** organization Al-Qaeda and its leader, Osama bin Laden. Al-Qaeda is the organization behind the terrorist attacks in the United States on 11th September 2001, as well as numerous other attacks. American and British forces have been searching for Al-Qaeda supporters and training camps in the mountains of Afghanistan ever since.

↑ The rugged mountains of the High Atlas in Morocco are the most westerly mountains in the region, and some of the more accessible. They are inhabited by a people known as Berbers.

People

In 2006 the population of the Middle East and North Africa was about 470 million people. This is relatively small in comparison with other regions, and represents less than 7 percent of the world total. The most populous countries in the region were Egypt (79 million), Turkey (70.5 million), and Iran (68.8 million). By contrast, the least populated were Bahrain, Cyprus, and Qatar, with between 700,000 and 1 million people each.

One characteristic of this region is rapid population growth. The populations of Kuwait, the Palestinian Territories, and Yemen are growing by over 3 percent a year, compared to a world average of 1.14 percent. In Qatar and the United Arab Emirates the rates are over 4.5 percent per year – among the highest in the world. At these growth rates, the populations of several countries in the region will almost double between 2006 and 2050. The populations of Afghanistan, Iraq, Yemen, and the Palestinian Territories are expected to grow even faster. In Yemen it is predicted to grow by over 200 percent.

The dominance of a single language (Arabic) and religion (Islam) in the region might suggest that its population is not very diverse. This is not the case. For example, people in Lebanon, Iran, and Turkey have a more liberal understanding of Islam. This means they enjoy greater freedoms than in more conservative countries such as Saudi Arabia and Kuwait, where strict laws and cultural beliefs can limit freedoms, especially for women.

← A woman sells bangles at a market in Kabul, Afghanistan. A business like this would have been impossible under the strict Islamic laws of the Taliban.

High fertility

A major cause of the region's high population growth is a high **fertility rate** – the number of children a woman is expected to have during her lifetime. In 2006, the world average was 2.7 children per woman. The average for the Middle East and North Africa varies greatly within the region. In 2006 in Cyprus, for example, it was just 1.5 and in Turkey only 2.2 children. By contrast, in Yemen it was 6.2 and in Afghanistan 6.8 children – one of the highest rates in the world.

In the past, high fertility rates were balanced by high **mortality** (death) **rates**. Modern medicines and improvements in general standards of living have lowered mortality rates in recent decades. When fertility rates remain high, populations can grow very quickly. One of the main health improvements has been a decline in early childhood deaths. In Turkey, the mortality rate for children under 5 years old fell from 133 per 1,000 live births in 1980 to 32 per 1,000 in 2004. Algeria, Morocco, and Iran have also experienced similar dramatic improvements.

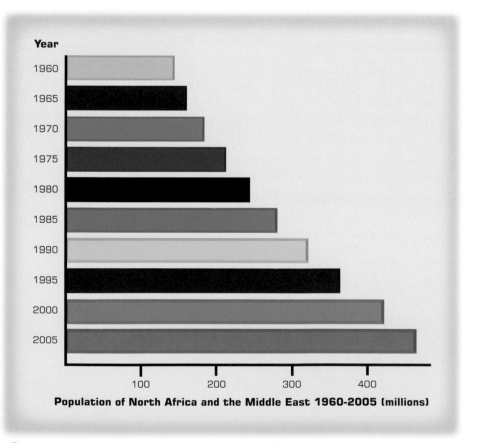

Population of North Africa and the Middle East 1960-2005 (millions)

This bar chart shows the growth in population in the Middle East and North Africa since 1960.

THE RIGHTS OF WOMEN

The rights of women are a major influence on population growth, and cultural traditions in parts of this region give women fewer rights than men. In many countries, for example, the movement of girls is limited once they reach puberty. They may be taken out of school, and forced into early marriages. With little education and control over who and when they marry, women can find themselves powerless to choose how many children to have. Large families are considered a status symbol in some parts of the region, so men may force their wives to have more children than they would want to.

Perhaps the most extreme example of limiting women's rights was the recent rule by the Taliban in Afghanistan (1996–2001). The education of all girls was banned, and many women were prevented from working outside their homes. Today, women's rights are the least recognized in the Gulf States, but are stronger in the countries bordering the Mediterranean such as Turkey, Lebanon, Israel, and Tunisia.

These girls are enjoying the benefits of education at a mixed gender school in Afghanistan. Until the fall of the Taliban, girls were denied such opportunities.

Youthful populations

The age structure of the region's population is very young. In Egypt, 35 percent of the population was under the age of 15 in 2006. In Afghanistan, Iraq, and Yemen this group was over 45 percent of the population. This compares to less than 20 percent of the population under the age of 15 in the United Kingdom, USA, or Australia. With such youthful populations, the overall population will continue growing rapidly for many years, even if fertility rates decline, because these young people will begin their own families. A youthful population also puts pressure on the government to meet the health and education needs of so many children. Essential resources such as water, already desperately short in many countries, also come under greater pressure.

Life expectancy

Improvements in healthcare over the last 50 years have greatly increased life expectancy in the region. In Algeria and Libya, for example, life expectancy at birth increased from 47 years for men and women in 1960, to 71 and 74 years respectively in 2005. As a whole, the region had a life expectancy at birth of 69 years in 2005. The world average was 67 years. In keeping with global trends, women in the region have a slightly longer life expectancy than men.

Israel has the highest life expectancy in the region, at 79 years. The lowest is found in countries that have recently suffered, or continue to suffer from conflict. In Yemen, for example, life expectancy is only 61. It is estimated to be even lower in Afghanistan and Iraq.

Education

Education levels vary considerably across the region, by both country and, in some areas, gender. Several countries, including Egypt, Israel, and Turkey, have prestigious universities that attract students from elsewhere in the region and beyond. For others, such as Afghanistan and Yemen, even providing primary schooling is an extreme challenge.

Differences in education level by gender show the inequalities between men and women in this region. In the region as a whole, 91 percent of boys will complete their primary education, but only 85 percent of girls will do so. The difference at secondary level education is even greater, as shown by the adult literacy figures (the percentage of those over 15 years old able to read and write). For the whole region, adult literacy for men is 82 percent, but for women just 62 percent. Literacy levels are much lower in some parts of the region. In Morocco, for example, 66 percent of men and just 40 percent of women are literate. In Afghanistan, the figures are 43 percent for men and 13 percent for women. Israel, Kuwait, Jordan, and Qatar, by contrast, have nearly 90 percent literacy for both men and women.

Health

The relatively healthy diets of the region mean people are generally in good health. Smoking is popular, however, so there is much smoking-related disease, but alcohol is strictly controlled or banned in much of the region. In poorer countries and communities, water-related diseases are linked to a lack of clean water supplies and sewerage. Children are especially vulnerable to these diseases, though simple lessons in hygiene can dramatically reduce the rate of illness.

The Middle East and North Africa has not yet experienced the high levels of **HIV** and **AIDS** that have devastated sub-Saharan Africa and parts of Asia. In 2005, there were around 110,000 people living with HIV or AIDS. This compares with around 25 million in sub-Saharan Africa. One of the major causes of HIV infection in the region is the sharing of infected needles by drug users.

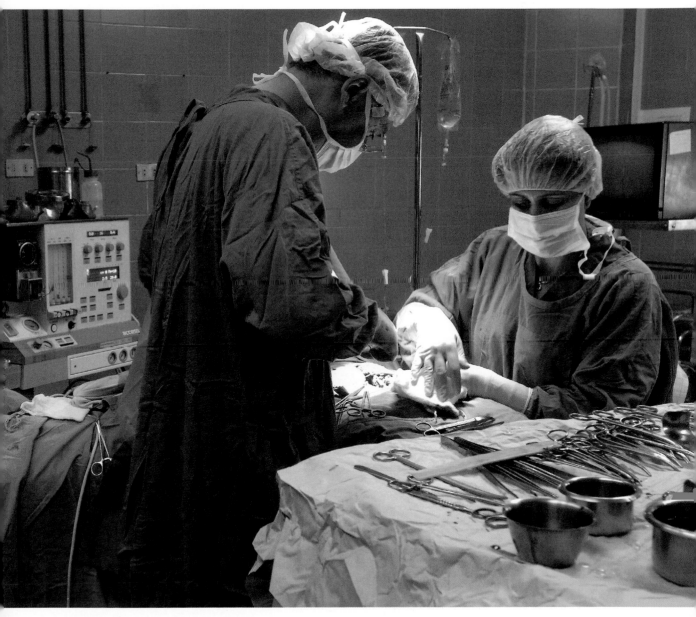

A woman is operated on in Adshee village, Lebanon, after being injured by a bomb. Hospitals in Lebanon are some of the best equipped in the region.

Urbanization

At the end of 2007, over half the world's population was living in urban centres, and the trend of **urbanization** continues. In common with this trend, the Middle East and North Africa is a rapidly urbanizing region. Most countries are already mainly urban. The exceptions are Afghanistan, where only 22 percent of the population lives in urban areas, Yemen where the figure is 26 percent, and Egypt where it is 43 percent. The most urbanized countries are Bahrain, Israel, Kuwait, and Qatar, where over 90 percent of the population is urban.

One reason for the region's high urbanization rate is the lack of productive farmland. Deserts and mountains are not suitable for farming and cannot support a rural population. Where farming is possible, such as in the Nile valley and delta in Egypt, population densities are extremely high, perhaps even higher than in some urban areas.

Istanbul is one of the most crowded and fastest growing cities in the region. Apartment blocks like these allow more people to fit into the city. They are replacing much of the lower density housing.

Mega cities

Mega cities are those with a population of over 10 million. According to the United Nations (UN), Cairo in Egypt was the region's first mega city. In 2005 its official population was 11.1 million, and it was one of only 20 official mega cities in the world. Most experts think the population of Cairo is much higher – up to 16 million if the surrounding suburbs are included. Istanbul in Turkey is the region's other mega city. It is impossible to calculate the population of the region's largest cities. In Istanbul hundreds of new immigrants arrive every day. The city is growing by over 200,000 people every year, creating problems for

GECEKONDU

As darkness falls in Istanbul, hundreds of newly arrived families set to work building themselves makeshift homes on vacant patches of land throughout the city. Known as gecekondu meaning 'built overnight', these homes are allowed to stay as long as they are finished by the morning. Over time people improve their gecekondu, but many are of poor quality and very vulnerable to earthquakes. It has been estimated that 65 percent of all buildings in Istanbul began as gecekondu, and that they house over half the population.

housing, traffic congestion, and the quality of the environment. People come to find jobs and a better standard of living, but many struggle to find work and end up in overcrowded housing. In Cairo, living conditions are so cramped that people even live in the city's cemetery, now known as the 'City of the Dead'. The Egyptian government has responded to the problem by building new cities in the surrounding desert. In Istanbul, the government is offering financial benefits to companies and people who move outside the main city. The experiences of Cairo and Istanbul will be closely watched by the region's other fast-growing cities, such as Tehran and Baghdad, which both had populations of around 7 million in 2005.

A devastating earthquake hit the city of Bam in December 2003, destroying much of the poor quality housing that families like this one were living in.

The Kreuzberg district of Berlin, Germany, is known for its large Turkish population. Turks are well integrated into Berlin's culture and economy as an established immigrant community.

On the move

The Middle East and North Africa has long been an area of high population mobility. Ancient trade routes across the Sahara desert helped to spread Arabic and Islam throughout the region. As these are now the common language and faith, movement within the region is relatively easy. People usually move in search of a higher income. The oil and gas industries of the Gulf States attract a large number of **migrant** workers. In 2004, for example, there were over 900,000 Egyptians working in Saudi Arabia. Altogether, migrants and their families make up almost half of Saudi Arabia's population.

Global migration

A growing number of migrant workers come from outside the region. The Gulf States of Bahrain, Kuwait, Qatar, Oman, Saudi Arabia, and the United Arab Emirates are particularly attractive to outsiders. The greatest number come from Asia, especially from Bangladesh, Pakistan, India, Sri Lanka, Indonesia, and the Philippines. Men often find work in industry or construction, while women take on domestic work. Most workers come alone and send money home to their families, in payments known as **remittances**. It is estimated that around US$1.2 billion is sent back to Sri Lanka in remittances each year, by the 730,000 Sri Lankans working in Saudi Arabia (350,000), the United Arab Emirates (160,000), Lebanon (80,000), Kuwait and Oman (40,000 in each), and Qatar and Jordan (30,000 in each).

This is an area of outward migration, too. Germany has a large Turkish community, for example. In Berlin there are about 120,000 Turkish residents and up to 180,000 more with Turkish origins. France has many people from North Africa (especially Algeria, Tunisia, and Morocco). One of the most famous is Zinedine Zidane, the captain of France's victorious 2002 World Cup football team, who has Algerian origins.

A Palestinian boy climbs as he tries to look through the concrete blocks of the imposing new security fence that separates the Gaza Strip from the rest of Israel.

Barriers to mobility

Israelis and Palestinians have been fighting over lands they both claim as theirs for over 50 years. In 2000, however, Palestinian-linked terrorist groups began to use suicide bombers to attack Israeli civilians in cities such as Jerusalem and Tel Aviv. In 2001, the Israeli government announced a new security fence to separate the Palestinian Territories from the rest of Israel. Israel says this is to prevent terrorist attacks, but the fence has been internationally criticized for blocking the mobility of Palestinians, who may have been cut off from work, study, or their families. The city of Jerusalem, which both Israelis and Palestinians claim as their capital, is particularly problematic. The security fence places it almost entirely within Israel.

SEEKING ASYLUM

In recent times, people have emigrated from the region to escape conflicts. Afghanistan, Iraq, Yemen, and the Palestinian Territories have seen this emigration. Many of these migrants arrive in Europe or North America as **refugees** seeking **asylum**. Recent **terrorist** attacks against western targets by people from North Africa and the Middle East have made these refugees not always welcome.

Governance and politics

Apart from Oman and Afghanistan, the countries of the Middle East and North Africa are politically young. Most gained their independence in the 1950s, some much later. Yemen, for example, only came into being in 1990 through a merger of the Yemen Arab Republic and the People's Democratic Republic of Yemen. Other countries have been through periods of great upheaval and only recently become more stable. Instability remains a problem in several countries, including Lebanon, Israel and the Palestinian territories, and Iraq.

Peace in the Middle East

One of the most serious challenges in the Middle East is the conflict between Israel and its Arab neighbours. Tensions have existed ever since Israel was created in 1948, and occasionally these erupt into full-blown conflict. Most recently, in 2006 Israel attacked Lebanon in retaliation for the kidnapping of an Israeli soldier by Lebanese **Hezbollah** fighters based there. Israel claimed that Syria was providing Hezbollah with financial support to launch attacks against Israel from Lebanon. Hundreds of innocent people died, and billions of dollars of damage was caused to Lebanese cities and transport networks.

Turkish UN peacekeepers check vehicles offloaded at Beirut in Lebanon. They are part of a peacekeeping force put in place in south Lebanon after the brief conflict between Lebanon and Israel in 2006.

There is considerable pressure from the international community for the countries of the Middle East to reach a lasting peace agreement. This would allow investment in the region and bring a better quality of life to its people. A so called 'road map' for peace negotiations has been suggested by the US government and supported by many others. It would offer an opportunity to develop the economy of the region, and benefit both Palestinians and Israelis. To date, however, it has been difficult to even get those involved in the dispute to sit at the same table. In January 2006 **Hamas**, a group closely associated with terrorist activities against Israel, won the parliamentary elections in the Palestinian Territories. Israel has refused to negotiate with the Palestinian Authority while it includes members of Hamas.

British soldiers in Basra, southern Iraq, talk to two men on a motorcycle in November 2006. The British have been in Iraq since the US-led invasion to remove Saddam Hussein in 2003.

FOREIGN INTERVENTION

The importance of the Middle East and North Africa to global trade and energy can make people suspicious about the motives of foreign governments who get involved in regional issues. Many think that the USA and United Kingdom only invaded Iraq in 2003 because they wanted to secure access to its huge oil reserves. The US and UK governments insisted that the invasion was to remove Saddam Hussein, a dangerous dictator with weapons of mass destruction (WMD). Over four years after their invasion, however, thousands of US and UK troops remained in Iraq, and the new government was unable to control the internal fighting that emerged after the fall of Saddam Hussein.

The US is openly critical of other nations in the region, including Syria and Iran, yet is a major supporter of Israel. This makes its involvement in the region even more complicated. One hopeful solution to tensions in the Middle East is the involvement of Turkey, which is considered a moderate country in the region. It is presently in negotiations to become a member of the European Union, but it also has strong political and cultural ties with the Arabic states of the Middle East. Turkey may be able to use this unique position to help the peace process.

Culture

Centuries of trade and population **migration**, together with a long history of invading forces, have made the Middle East and North Africa a culturally diverse region. These factors have also carried many traditions from the region around the world. This is how Christianity and Islam spread from this region to become the dominant faiths in the world. Ideas of design, food, science, literature, and the arts have also spread far and wide. Many buildings in the western world incorporate elements of the region's architecture and design. The strong use of geometric shapes in Islamic art has also influenced garden design around the world.

Though incredibly diverse and continuing to change, there are some common features of culture in the region. The most obvious are the dominant language (Arabic) and religion (Islam), but there are others. Close family ties are important, and extended families often live and work in close proximity. Eating out is a popular social event, and in many parts people wear similar cool, flowing garments to suit the hot climate. Elements of the arts and sports are also shared and enjoyed across the region.

← The Grand Mosque at Kairouan in Tunisia, North Africa, is a UNESCO World Heritage Site.

Centres of religion

Three of the world's major religions trace their origins to North Africa and the Middle East. This gives parts of the region great spiritual significance. Mecca in Saudi Arabia is the centre of the Muslim world and Islam's holiest site. Bethlehem in the Palestinian Territories is heralded as the birthplace of Jesus and is important to Christians all over the world. Nowhere, however, can compare with Jerusalem for its religious importance. Jerusalem is the holiest site for both Judaism and Christianity, and the third most important site in Islam (after Mecca and Medina).

For Jews, the remnants of their second temple (built in 515 BCE), known as the Western or 'Wailing' Wall, form the holiest site in Judaism. Jewish pilgrims from all over the world visit every day. Worshippers insert prayers or wishes, written on tiny pieces of paper, into gaps between the wall's stones. For Christians the Church of the Holy Sepulchre is the most holy site. It was originally built in 326 CE on what is believed to be the site of Jesus' crucifixion. For Muslims, the Dome of the Rock on Hara mesh-Sharif (Temple Mount) is the holiest site in Jerusalem, and the third holiest in Islam. It houses a rock from which the prophet Mohammed is believed to have made his night journey to pray with God.

In Mecca, Saudi Arabia, Muslim pilgrims circle the Kaaba, the holy relic of Islam, as part of their Haj.

The Western or Wailing Wall in Jerusalem is a sacred site of Judaism, because it is the closest place to the site of the ancient Jewish temple that stood where the Dome of the Rock (visible behind it) was built.

Religious composition

Islam is followed by over 80 percent of the population in all countries of the region except Cyprus, Israel, and Lebanon. In 12 of the 22 countries, more than 90 percent of the population are Muslims, with Yemen the highest at 99.9 percent. Christianity is the next biggest religion, though it is only observed by a significant part of the population in Cyprus and Lebanon. Judaism is the dominant faith in Israel (which was founded in 1948 as a Jewish state), where it is the faith of almost 80 percent of the population. It features little elsewhere, apart from in a small following in the neighbouring Palestinian Territories.

Hinduism is practised by economic migrants in the Gulf States. Zoroastrianism is an ancient religion from Persia (now Iran) that follows the teachings of Zoroaster from around 1200 BCE. Most followers moved to India following Muslim conquests of Persia, but a sizeable number can still be found in Iran today. Another faith with origins in Iran is the Bahá'í faith, centred on the beliefs of Baha'u'llah. The spiritual centre of the Bahá'í is Haifa in Israel, however, near to where Baha'u'llah later lived and died. The Bahá'í faith was only founded in 1844, and is one of the world's newest major religions. It is unusual because it accepts and welcomes all other religions, seeking to build unity between all beliefs for the common good of humanity.

LANGUAGE SURVIVAL

With the common use of Arabic and business languages such as French and English, some of the region's lesser languages are under threat. One of these is Aramaic, an ancient language that some believe was used by Jesus. Once the main regional language, it was replaced by Arabic and is now considered endangered. It is spoken only by scattered communities in the region, and now has many different variations.

In contrast to Aramaic, Hebrew is an ancient language that was virtually extinct until it was revitalized by Ben Yehuda. Arriving in Israel in 1881, Yehuda took ancient biblical Hebrew and turned it into a living language, by creating new words to describe more modern aspects of life such as cars and electricity. He used only Hebrew to speak to other people, and in time his passion for the language influenced others to speak it. Hebrew is today the main language of Israel.

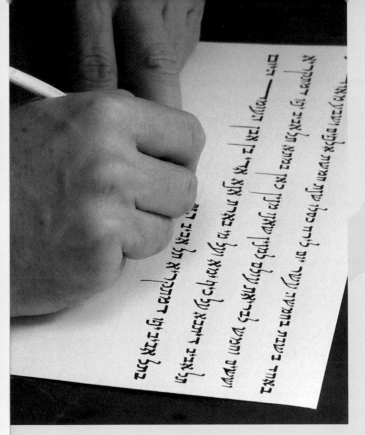

↑ The Hebrew language being written here almost became extinct, before its revival in the early 20th century.

Culture and the arts

With much of the region sharing both religion and language, distinctive regional traditions and arts have also emerged. Some, such as belly dancing, have become popular beyond the region, others have remained more local, such as camel racing (popular in the Arabian peninsula) and the unique Afghan sport of *buzkashi*. *Buzkashi* is hundreds of years old, and is played by teams of men on horseback. The game involves trying to score a goal by pitching the carcass of a dead goat across a goal line (*buzkashi* means 'goat killing'). It is a fast and physical game, and players are frequently injured.

Music

Music, and particularly singing, has been an important part of Arabic culture for centuries. Some of the biggest Arab stars are said to be more influential than political leaders. Singing and music come from a long tradition of poetry in the region, so the words of songs in Arabic are generally more important than the music. Arabic singing is particularly known for its haunting, emotional voices that cover an incredible range of tones. Music is not part of the Islamic faith, as early Islamic scholars associated it with undesirable activities and banned it. Nevertheless, the call to prayer by the *muezzin* uses the Arabic scales (called 'maqamat') upon which Arabic music is based. A group of Islamic mystics known as '*sufis*' have ignored the mainstream exclusion of music from Islam. They use music as a way to communicate with God, and perform a whirling dance called the *suki*. They enter a trance-like state that allows them to talk with God. *Sufi* music and dancing is still practised today in Turkey and Egypt.

Members of the *sufi* whirling dervishes perform their rhythmic and entrancing dance, in Cairo, Egypt. They believe the dance brings them closer to God.

Classical Arabic music, using vocals and instruments such as the *nay* (flute), *darbuka* (drum), *duff* (tambourine) and *ud* (lute), remains hugely popular in the region, but modern music is also emerging. Arabic street pop, known as *Al-jil*, first emerged in the 1970s in Egypt and began to mix Arabic traditions with modern electrical instruments and dance rhythms. A popular mix of Arabic, folk, and modern music also emerged in Turkey, called *Arabesk*. This and Egyptian street pop are the main forms of popular music in the region today.

Cinema

As in music, Egypt dominates the film industry of the region, producing about 15 new films a year. Morocco, Syria, Turkey, Iran, and Israel have smaller film industries. The region is also a popular location for movie-makers from Hollywood. The *Star Wars* films and the English film *The English Patient* were filmed in the dramatic desert landscapes of Tunisia.

Food and diet

Regional diets are influenced by religion. Both Islam and Judaism have strict dietary guidelines, such as a ban on the eating of pork. Jewish dietary rules (known as kosher diet) also ban non-scaly fish, so that shellfish and squid, for example, are not eaten. The religions also dictate the way food should be prepared. The Koran states that all meat must be slaughtered and drained of blood in a particular way. The result is known as *halal* meat. The preparation of meat also has specific rules in Judaism, known as *shehita*. These include preparing, cooking, and eating meat separately from dairy products, with completely different sets of cutlery, crockery, and utensils.

← The kebab, the most famous of the region's foods, has become popular around the world. A true kebab consists of small pieces of meat on a skewer, roasted over a fire. Kebabs are thought to originate from Turkey.

A fish market in Istanbul sells the morning's fresh catch. Fish forms an important part of the diet in the region, especially in coastal areas.

Quick snacks and street food are popular throughout the region, such as *falafel* (deep-fried balls of chickpeas mixed with herbs and spices) and kebabs. More hearty meals are often based on a meat or vegetable stew eaten with rice, pasta, or local forms of bread. Another typical dish is the *mezze*, which is any meal made up of several small dishes rather than one main one. A *mezze* can include 10 or more dishes, including local delicacies such as *hummus* (a chickpea-based paste) and *taboulah* (salad of cracked wheat, tomato, lemon, and olives). Green salad and flat bread (variations of pitta bread) normally accompany a *mezze*.

These men are enjoying smoking a water pipe while playing board games in a coffee house at Na'ama Bay, Sharm el Sheikh, Egypt.

The coffee house

The coffee house is central to social life across much of the region. They have formed meeting places for hundreds of years, though only men can go there in the stricter Islamic states. Besides strong coffee (an Arabic favourite), tea, juices, snacks, and sweet pastries are served. People also play social games there such as dominoes, backgammon, or cards, and enjoy the social smoking of a *sheesha* (also known as *nargile* or *hookah*). This is a water pipe that is used to smoke flavoured tobacco. It does not contain the harmful chemicals of cigarettes, and uses relatively little tobacco.

Natural resources and economy

The economies of the Middle East and North Africa range from the extreme poverty of post-war Afghanistan, to the enormous wealth of the oil-rich Gulf States such as Kuwait and Saudi Arabia. In Kuwait, for example, the average annual income of US$24,040 in 2005 was over 21 times greater than in the Palestinian Territories. The richest states in the region, in terms of the value of their total economy, are Turkey, Saudi Arabia, and Iran. According to the World Bank these were the 20th, 22nd and 31st wealthiest nations in the world in 2005.

The energy industry is by far the most important economic activity in the region, but it is certainly not the only creator of wealth. The region is well known for its specialist agricultural produce such as dried fruits and spices, and has long been a world leader in textiles. More recently, tourism has become a major growth industry in several parts of the region. Dubai, in the United Arab Emirates, is an interesting example of this recent shift in the economy. Massive construction projects are helping to create an entire new economy in Dubai based on leisure, shopping, and international business.

The region has an enormous influence on global trade. Countries of the region control key trading routes such as the Suez Canal in Egypt and the Bosporus Strait in Turkey. These regulate the flow of trade between Europe, Asia, and Africa, and onwards with the rest of the world. There are also important road and rail networks that head east towards the growing economic superpowers of China and India. It is the region's oil wealth that gives it the greatest influence on global trade, however. When this power has been used in the past it has caused major world crises (see page 47).

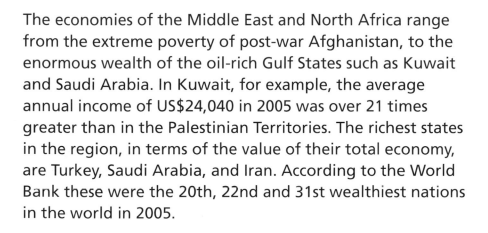

← A vast network of pipes carries crude oil to a refinery (in the background) at Dharam in Saudi Arabia.

Black gold

Oil is sometimes called 'black gold' because of its enormous economic value. Few economies in the world could function without it, and many of the world's wealthiest economies rely heavily on it to meet their energy needs. Across the world, even small changes in the price of oil can have an enormous impact.

The region dominates the global trade in oil. In 2005 it produced 36.3 percent of the world's oil – an amazing 29.6 million barrels of oil every day. Saudi Arabia is by far the largest producer, but other major producers include Iran, Kuwait, United Arab Emirates, and Iraq. More significant than production levels are the region's enormous reserves of oil. In 2006 the region had around 800 thousand million barrels of oil, or two thirds of the world's reserves.

Natural gas

Natural gas, also found in the region, is a cleaner fuel than oil. It is used for generating electricity, in industrial processes, and for domestic heating and cooking. In 2005, the region produced 15.5 percent of the world's natural gas. The main producers were Algeria, Iran, and Saudi Arabia. Like oil, however, it is the region's reserves of natural gas that are most significant. There is more natural gas here than anywhere else in the world – 44.5 percent of global proven reserves in 2006. Most of this is in Iran (14.9 percent) and Qatar (14.3 percent).

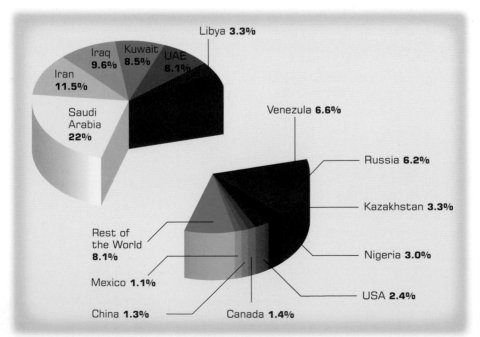

← This pie chart shows the percentages of the world's proven oil reserves held by the countries of the region in 2006.

OPEC AND THE PRICE OF OIL

In 1960, a group of oil-producing countries formed a group called the Organization of the Petroleum Exporting Countries, or OPEC for short. OPEC is made up of 11 countries and all except Indonesia, Nigeria, and Venezuela are in this region. OPEC members meet to agree oil production levels for each member country. Their decisions can influence the price of oil in the world markets. If they reduce production there can be supply shortages, causing oil prices to rise. If production is increased, prices tend to fall. OPEC regulates production to keep world prices stable and protect its members – all of whom are heavily dependent on oil exports for their income.

In October 1973, following Israeli attacks on Arab neighbours during the Arab-Israeli war, OPEC members stopped oil exports to all countries that showed support for Israel. The sudden shortage in oil supplies sent prices soaring, creating an 'oil crisis'. The crisis lasted until March 1974, when OPEC removed its block on exports. Another crisis occurred in 1979, when a revolution in Iran led to a sudden fall in oil production.

This ability to influence world oil supplies makes the region very powerful, although today other oil-producing countries such as Mexico, Russia, Canada, and Norway can help to balance world supplies. OPEC members still have the largest oil reserves, however, and so may become more powerful again in the future.

Giant oil storage tanks at Yanbu in the desert of Saudi Arabia form part of the country's enormous oil-producing infrastructure.

Global connections

The energy wealth of the Middle East and North Africa has given it trade connections across the world. Pipelines transport gas from the region into homes and industries in Europe, and enormous tankers transport oil to the USA, Europe, Japan, Australia and beyond. The region was a centre of global trading long before this trade in energy developed, however. From about 200 BCE a famous trade route called the 'silk road'

The Suez Canal is an essential artery for trade into and out of the region, and beyond.

connected modern day Turkey with China, passing through Iran and Afghanistan. It consisted of several routes across the region, and linked traders in the Mediterranean region with Arabia, Russia, India, and China. Goods traded along the route included spices, gold, precious stones, and ivory, as well as silk from China. The silk road was largely replaced from the 16th century by shipping, which became cheaper than transporting goods by land.

It is shipping that dominates trade in the region today. The Bosporus Strait in Turkey and the Suez Canal in Egypt are both essential shipping channels. As well as oil, these routes are essential for carrying agricultural, manufactured and industrial goods into and out of the region.

A new silk route

There is new interest in recreating the silk route through a series of modern road and rail projects. These would combine to create land-based trading routes across the region. Turkey, for example, is building a new tunnel under the Bosporus that would allow non-stop rail travel between Europe and Asia. A new route could provide countries such as Afghanistan with much needed economic growth.

TAPPING CASPIAN RESOURCES

The Caspian Sea, to the north of Iran, borders several countries in central Asia. Discoveries of new oil and gas reserves under the Caspian Sea have led to a rush to extract and export them. In May 2005, a new oil pipeline was opened stretching over 1600 kilometres (994 miles) from the Caspian port of Baku in Azerbaijan to the Turkish port of Ceyhan. The BTC (Baku-T'bilisi-Ceyhan) pipeline will deliver up to a million barrels of oil per day to Ceyhan, from where it will be shipped by tanker. A gas pipeline will follow a similar route and deliver Caspian gas to Turkey and through Greece to western Europe.

Other pipelines are likely to follow, but the debate is whether they should go west towards Europe, or south and east to meet the growing energy demands of Asia, especially China and India. One likely route is through Afghanistan to the growing economies of Pakistan and India. Another route is through Iran to the Persian Gulf, from where it can be shipped. Political stability in the region is a major obstacle, as pipelines are vulnerable to attack. Few companies will invest the billions of dollars needed to build these pipelines until the region is more secure.

This factory in the Palestine Occupied Territories of Israel produces textiles, one of the main manufacturing industries in the region.

Manufacturing

A wide range of manufactured goods are produced in the region. Textiles are important, particularly in Turkey, Morocco, Tunisia, and Egypt. In 2003, Turkey was the world's fourth largest producer of clothing and tenth largest producer of non-clothing textiles. Textiles account for about 20 percent of Turkey's manufacturing labour, 30 percent of its export income, and 10 percent of its total income. Food-based products are another key area of manufacturing. Fruits and nuts are often processed or dried before being exported. Processed vegetables and fish products are also exported, mainly to Europe and within the region. Turkey, Egypt, Iran, Syria, Morocco, Israel, Jordan, and Tunisia all have significant food processing industries.

High-tech manufacturing

High technology industries include the manufacture of electronics, automobiles, household appliances, and chemicals. International manufacturers of these goods invest in the region, because of its well educated and relatively low-cost labour force. Israel has long been a producer of high-tech manufactured goods using modern, computerized processes. In recent years, Turkey has developed a substantial automotive and home appliances industry, and in 2003 produced about 5 percent of the world's televisions. Countries such as Kuwait, Saudi Arabia, and United Arab Emirates use their oil and gas reserves to produce a variety of chemical and other oil-based products.

Service industries

Services such as banking, insurance, data processing, and travel are a growing sector of the region's economies. Dubai, in the United Arab Emirates, is a good example of this. Many new office blocks, hotels and conference facilities are being built. The Middle East has advantages for service industries because it is located between the time-zones of Asia and Europe. It can provide a link between these major markets and service their needs. The region's location has advantages for the travel industry, too. Dubai is a fast-growing air hub for international passenger and cargo traffic. Aden, in Yemen, is hoping to achieve the same with international shipping, as it stands at the meeting point of the Red Sea (leading to the Suez Canal) and the Indian Ocean. New container-handling facilities opened there in 1999, and by 2006 the volume of containers handled had more than trebled.

Tourism

Tourism is the world's fastest growing industry, as cheaper air travel makes it accessible to more people. The region has benefited considerably from this. In Egypt the number of tourists increased from around 2.4 million per year in 1990 to 5.1 million in 2000. Tunisia saw tourist numbers increase from 3.2 to 5.1 million over the same period. The United Arab Emirates had the most impressive growth, from just 0.6 million in 1990 to 3.9 million in 2000. Overall, the region accounted for 9 percent of all international tourism in 2005. It is forecast to be the world's fastest growing tourism region up to 2020, with average growth of 7.1 percent a year.

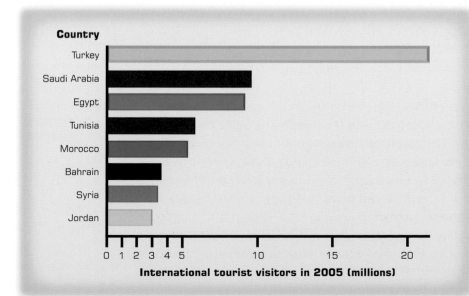

← This bar chart shows the number of international tourists visiting the leading countries in the region in 2005.

Inequality and poverty

A continuing issue for the Middle East and North Africa is the fact that its oil wealth is not equally distributed. A few very wealthy families and individuals control not just the oil industry, but in some countries the entire economy, even the country. In Saudi Arabia, the Saud family who founded the modern state in 1932 dominate the country and its oil. They have amassed enormous personal wealth, while between 13 and 25 percent of Saudi men remain unemployed. In Egypt, too, there is an obvious divide between rich and poor. Luxury riverside mansions in Cairo's upmarket neighbourhoods house the businessmen, film and music stars of the Arabic world. Just a short distance away, some of the poorest people in the world are sleeping under bridges or on rickety boats moored to the banks of the Nile. They survive by begging or scavenging for waste to sell for recycling.

Luxury limousines parked outside one of the many new business hotels that have opened in Dubai in recent years.

Informal economy

One outcome of these inequalities is a booming **informal economy**. This is where people earn cash for jobs and services they provide, but they are not officially employed or taxed. In Turkey, the informal economy plays a major role in the textile industry. Thousands of people, mostly women, work from home making garments for very low pay. They sell them on to the major companies, who export them to Europe and elsewhere. In other parts of the region, informal workers might be tourist guides, waste collectors, or shoe-shiners. Many governments tolerate informal workers because they provide important services, but as this sector is not regulated people can be forced to work in poor or dangerous conditions, for very low pay.

Crime

Great inequalities in wealth often lead to problems of crime, but crime levels in this region are relatively low. This is partly explained by the power of the Islamic faith, that severely punishes those who commit crimes. In less strict societies, such as in Turkey, crime rates have been rising slowly, though much of this has been minor thefts targeting wealthy tourists. The most serious crimes are committed by the organized terrorist groups, who occasionally launch bombing attacks to protest against the actions of other groups or governments.

Regional aid

Some of the region's wealth is redistributed through aid. Saudi Arabia, for example, is a major donor and has provided aid to several of its neighbouring countries. Since 2000, the Saudi government has given or promised over US$307 million to the occupied Palestinian Territories, and US$230 million to Afghanistan. In addition, Saudi Arabia has promised over US$1 billion worth of loans and trade guarantees to help Iraq rebuild its economy. Another major aid provider is the United Arab Emirates and its Abu Dhabi Fund for Development (ADFD). The ADFD has given more than US$5.4 billion since 1971 to over 56 countries, many within the region, including Morocco, Tunisia, Egypt, Jordan, Lebanon, and Yemen. ADFD focuses funding on food production projects and tourism investment, but also funds health, water, transport, and energy projects.

These men offering shoe repairs on the street in Afghanistan are part of the informal economy of the region. They offer a valuable service, but pay no taxes.

A Palestinian worker and farmer are watched by an Israeli soldier at a checkpoint in Habla, near the border between Israel and the Palestinian Territories.

Future prospects

The Middle East and North Africa is a region with great prospects for the future. Its vast energy reserves mean it will have great influence with the rest of the world, which is fast running out of energy supplies. Furthermore, the region could also be a major producer of new forms of energy, such as solar power and hydrogen-based fuels. It could use its solar power (readily available in the sunny desert) to convert seawater from the surrounding oceans into clean-burning hydrogen fuel – the fuel that many experts believe will one day replace petrol and diesel in our vehicles.

Closer ties

The region is developing closer ties with other parts of the world, through trade and population **migration**. This is bringing new ideas to the region, some of which challenge traditional ways of life. Migrant workers may be used to drinking alcohol, for example, which is forbidden in Islamic culture. In countries such as the United Arab Emirates, with a large population of migrant workers, there are signs that the rules are being ignored and drinking alcohol is becoming commonplace, even a problem. Turkey is in a unique position within the region, as it is currently negotiating to become part of the European Union (EU). Turkey has the largest economy of the region, and is a major cultural and economic influence. The success or failure of its bid to join the EU could bring considerable changes to the region, especially in relation to trade.

Peace and stability

The most serious issue facing the region is the struggle for national and regional peace. Israel is still engaged in a serious struggle with its Arab neighbours over their shared claims to land. Afghanistan and Iraq are trying to rebuild democratic governments, after years of interference and brutal leadership. Both have international troops in their lands to help them in this process, but both are still experiencing violence and instability. Iran is key to the peace of the region, and the problem of its threats against Israel is combined with its activities in developing nuclear technology. The Iranian government claims this nuclear programme is only for the peaceful generation of electricity. Not everyone believes them, however. Some, including the US, UK and Israeli governments, fear that Iran could try to develop nuclear weapons.

International co-operation

The key to the future of the region is greater international co-operation. Governments around the world are keen to see the region find peaceful solutions to its problems, and to avoid a global energy crisis or major conflict. Unfortunately the history of the Middle East and North Africa has been one of continual conquest by outside forces. Each time, these forces have left their mark in some way and made the region the fascinating mix of cultures and peoples that it is today. Now the different groups with an interest in the region must come together for peaceful reasons, and find a way to work together for a common future.

Gleaming new skyscrapers emerge from what was once desert in the fast growing city of Dubai – a symbol of the hopeful future for the region.

Fact file

Countries of the region

Country/Territory	capital	area sq km (sq miles)	population
Afghanistan	Kabul	652,090 (251,773)	32,253,000
Algeria	Algiers	2,381,740 (919,595)	34,355,000
Bahrain	Manama	710 (274)	722,000
Cyprus	Nicosia	9,251 (3,572)	853,000
Egypt	Cairo	1,001,449 (386,662)	77,243,000
Iran	Tehran	1,648,195 (636,372)	72,048,000
Iraq	Baghdad	438,317 (169,235)	30,958,000
Israel	Jerusalem*	22,145 (8,550)	7,250,000
Jordan	Amman	89,342 (34,495)	5,816,000
Kuwait	Kuwait	17,818 (6,880)	2,895,000
Lebanon	Beirut	10,400 (4,015)	3,894,000
Libya	Tripoli	1,759,540 (679,362)	6,266,000
Morocco	Rabat	446,550 (172,414)	31,851,000
Oman	Muscat	309,500 (119,499)	2,705,000
Palestinian Territories	Jerusalem*	360 (139) Gaza 5,860 (2,261) West Bank	1,482,405 Gaza 2,535,927 West Bank
Qatar	Doha	11,000 (4,247)	841,000
Saudi Arabia	Riyadh	2,149,690 (830,000)	26,362,000
Syria	Damascus	185,180 (71,498)	20,423,000
Turkey	Ankara	783,562 (302,535)	71,158,467
United Arab Emirates	Abu Dhabi	83,600 (32,278)	4,724,000
Tunisia	Tunis	163,610 (63,170)	10,352,000
Yemen	Sanaa	527,968 (203,850)	23,054,000

Population figures are estimates for 2008
* Both Israel and the Palestinian Territories claim Jerusalem as their capital.

Timeline

c.6000 BCE	Some of the earliest known civilizations in the world begin to form in Mesopotamia.
c.3100 BCE	The Ancient Egyptians create a thriving civilization centre on the River Nile in Egypt.
c.3000 BCE	The great Sumerian cities of Ur and Kish are built in what is now Iraq.
515 BCE	The Second Temple is built in Jerusalem.
332 BCE	Alexander the Great conquers Egypt, ending the Ancient Egyptian civilization before going on to conquer much of the region.
c.200 BCE	The Silk Road forms an important trade route through the region, connecting Europe to China. It survives until the 1700s.
326 CE	The Church of the Holy Sepulchre is constructed in Jerusalem on the site where Jesus is believed to have been crucified.
1844	The Bahá'í faith is founded.
1881	Ben Yehuda arrives in Israel and begins the revival of the Hebrew language – today the national language of Israel – and turned it into a living language.
1932	The Saud family found the modern state of Saudi Arabia. They remain the ruling family.
1948	Israel is founded as a Jewish state following the withdrawal of the British from their control of what was Palestine.
1956	Egypt seizes control of the Suez Canal, prompting a brief conflict with Britain, France, and Israel.
1960	The Organization of Petroleum Exporting Countries (OPEC) is founded.
1970	The Aswan High Dam is completed across the Nile river to supply electricity to Egypt and prevent the annual flooding.
1973–74	OPEC causes an oil crisis when it blockades supplies of oil to western countries who supported Israel in the Arab-Israeli war.

1984	Libya begins work on its Great Man Made River project. It will be completed in 2025.
1995	A Jewish extremist assassinates the Israeli prime minister, Yitzak Rabin, for his tolerant attitude to the Palestinians.
2001	Islamic extremist terrorists linked to Al-Qaeda attack targets in the US in New York and Washington, including the famous twin towers of New York.
2001	Israel announces the start of a security fence/wall to separate Israeli territory from that controlled by the Palestinian authorities.
2002	The Taliban are removed from power in Afghanistan by an international force led by the US.
2003	Forces led by the US and UK invade Iraq to overthrow Saddam Hussein, who they believed was developing weapons of mass destruction.
2003	An earthquake destroys most of the Iranian city of Bam, killing at least 27,000 people.
2004	Cyprus joins the European Union (EU), the first nation from the region to do so. Turkey is currently engaged in discussions to join.
2005	The BTC (Baku-T'bilisi-Ceyhan) oil pipeline is opened from the Caspian port of Baku in Azerbaijan to the Turkish port of Ceyhan.
2006	Hamas wins parliamentary elections in the Palestinian Territories. Israel refuses to talk to any government that includes Hamas.
2006	Israel invades Lebanon in retaliation for the kidnapping of an Israeli soldier by Hezbollah members operating there.

Glossary

aquifer	underground reservoir of water. Aquifers provide a valuable source of water throughout the world and are especially important in desert environments.
asylum	the seeking of safety from violence or persecution by fleeing to another country
burqa	garment, normally blue or black, that covers a woman from head to toe, with only an opening for her eyes. It is worn over other clothing.
delta	section of a river where it slows and spreads out (often in a triangular pattern) before meeting the sea
desalination	process by which salts are removed from saltwater to make it useable for human consumption or for growing crops
ecosystem	the contents of an environment, including all the plants and animals that live there. This could be a garden pond, a forest, or the whole Earth.
evaporation	process by which water turns from a liquid to gas form. Evaporation is much higher in hot climates.
fertility rate	number of children an average woman in any given society will have during her lifetime
global warming	process in which the average air temperature of the atmosphere is rising
Hamas	political party and military force based in the Palestinian Territories, that formed in the late 1980s. It is opposed to Israeli occupation of what it considers Palestinian lands.
Hezbollah	political party and military force based in Lebanon, that formed in the 1980s to end the occupation of southern Lebanon by Israeli forces
HIV/AIDS	Human Immunodeficiency Virus (HIV) is a deadly virus spread by unprotected sex or contaminated needles or blood supplies. It can develop into Acquired Immuno-Deficiency Syndrome (AIDS) which is fatal. Expensive drugs can keep people alive, but there is no cure.
informal economy	the unregulated and often unknown part of an economy. The informal sector is dominated by small scale, cash-based businesses that avoid paying taxes.
irrigation	the artificial application of water for cultivating crops in areas or seasons of low or unreliable rainfall
lapse rate	used to describe the cooling of average air temperatures that occurs due to an increase in altitude

literate	able to read and write
migrant	someone who moves or has moved from one area to another (migration). This can occur within or between countries.
militia	military force, often made up of civilians
mortality rate	the number of people per thousand in the population who die in any particular period
orthodox	having very strong traditional beliefs
peninsula	piece of land that juts out into the sea
pharaoh	a ruler (king) of the Ancient Egyptians
refugee	person fleeing their home due to conflict or natural pressures and seeking refuge elsewhere, often in another country
remittance	payment made to family and friends in a home country, by workers living overseas
salinization	process whereby soils become increasingly saline due to contamination with dissolved salts from over-watering. It is normally associated with poor irrigation management.
strait	narrow body of water that connects two larger bodies of water
Taliban	political and military group that believe in an extreme form of Islam and enforce this on those they control. The Taliban ruled Afghanistan between 1996 and 2002.
terrorist	someone who commits unprovoked and illegal acts of violence against others, often innocent victims
urbanization	process by which a population becomes increasingly concentrated into urban centres (towns and cities)

Find out more

Further reading

World In Focus: Afghanistan, Nikki van der Gaag (Wayland, 2007)

World In Focus: Turkey, Anita Ganeri (Wayland, 2007)

World In Focus: Israel, Alex Woolf (Wayland, 2007)

World In Focus: Egypt, Jen Green and Nicola Barber (Wayland, 2007)

Great Cities of the World: Cairo, Rob Bowden and Roy Maconachie (World Almanac, 2005)

Great Cities of the World: Jerusalem, Rob Bowden (World Almanac, 2006)

Great Cities of the World: Baghdad, Nikki van der Gaag (World Almanac, 2006)

Global Cities: Istanbul, Rob Bowden (Evans Brothers, 2007)

Rivers Through Time: Settlements of the Indus, Rob Bowden (Heinemann Library, 2005)

Rivers Through Time: Settlements of the River Nile, Rob Bowden (Heinemann Library, 2005)

Websites

http://news.bbc.co.uk/1/hi/world/middle_east/default.stm
The BBC pages focussing on the Middle East provide a useful first point of research for information on the region.

http://news.bbc.co.uk/1/hi/in_depth/middle_east/2001/israel_and_the_ palestinians/default.stm
The BBC page focussing on the conflict between Israel and the Palestinians.

http://web.worldbank.org/WBSITE/EXTERNAL/COUNTRIES/MENAEXT/
The World Bank Middle East and North Africa site includes information on up to date development issues, such as the problems of water shortages and poverty.

www.opec.org/home
Learn all about OPEC and how it is able to influence the world supply and price of oil.

www.bbc.co.uk/religion/religions
A useful site for explaining the background to many of the world's major religions, including the main ones found in the Middle East and North Africa.

Activities

Here are some topics to research if you want to find out more about the Middle East and North Africa:

• Conflict in the Middle East
What is the origin of the conflict between Israel and its neighbours? Why has peace been so difficult to find? Who is involved in the peace process? A good place to start research is: http://news.bbc.co.uk/1/hi/in_depth/middle_east/2001/israel_and_the_palestinians/default.stm

• Water shortages
Water is in very short supply in many parts of the region. What plans are being made to improve water supplies? Could water shortages really lead to war in the region? Start your research at: http://news.bbc.co.uk/1/hi/in_depth/world/2003/world_forum/water/default.stm

Index